Pakenham Thomas Beatty

Spretae Carmina Musae

First Series: Songs of Love and Death

Pakenham Thomas Beatty

Spretae Carmina Musae
First Series: Songs of Love and Death

ISBN/EAN: 9783337006914

Printed in Europe, USA, Canada, Australia, Japan

Cover: Foto ©Thomas Meinert / pixelio.de

More available books at **www.hansebooks.com**

FIRST SERIES :

SONGS OF LOVE AND DEATH

BY

PAKENHAM BEATTY.

"A common folk I walk among ;
I speak dull things in their own tongue :
But all the while within I hear
A song I do not sing for fear—
How sweet, how different a thing !
And when I come where none are near
I open all my heart aud sing."
ARTHUR O'SHAUGHNESSY.

LONDON :

GEORGE BELL & SONS, YORK ST., COVENT GARDEN,

AND NEW YORK.

1893.

Dedication.

To ROBERT BROWNING.

NONE love in vain; for God, who will not take
His least gift back, takes not this heavenliest one ;
None of his faithful will Love's heart forsake
Though death make dumb the spring and dark the sun.

The dead are always with us everywhere,
Unseen of mortal eyes, yet unremoved,
Those gracious ghosts that make the twilight fair,
The souls that lighted ours, and hearts that loved.

No nightingale sings for the rose alone,
But the least leaf may share his gift of song ;
So, while the many mourners make their moan,
I, least of all who loved thee, shall not wrong

Thy fame, when these have left thee with thy peers,
Nor of thy spirit be misunderstood
That bring thee my Love's gift of song and tears—
I give my best, and each heart's best is good.

CONTENTS.

ERRATA.

Page 32, line 1, *for* " there is " *read* " there's."
Page 70, line 3, *for* " and splendid," etc. *read* " and
   splendid and sonorous spheres."
Page 121, line 6, *for* " life " *read* " love."

b

CONTENTS.

b

viii CO.NTENTS.

CONTENTS.

"The work of our hands, Lord, establish Thou it."

PILGRIMAGE.

B

PILGRIMAGE.

I.

SPRING smiles, as Hope that looks on Love,
On April buds grown flowers of May ;
A golden glory from above
Makes bright dim walks where lovers stray :
I turn my face another way

Until I reach that place apart
My holiest thoughts have made divine,
Bring forth the treasures of my heart
And deck the altar, pour the wine,
And worship at my soul's pure shrine.

No pleasant paths lead to that place,
No singing of glad birds is sweet
Along that way ; against my face
The keen hail strikes, the wild winds beat,
And sharp stones bruise my wearied feet.

And there is none on that dark way
To speak one word of hope or cheer ;
And none of all I meet will stay,
But all pass by me, swift as Fear
That sees an enemy draw near.

I lie down on some lonely heath,
And close my eyes against the light :
My sleep starts from some dream of death,
And wild beasts fill me with affright,
Their fierce eyes gleaming through the night.

But I keep on until I gain
That place, and kneel, and pray my prayer :
And know my praying is not vain,
And find my days less hard to bear
For that brief hour I worship there.

II.

COME, kneel down by the grave where Love is
  laid,
And pluck away the weeds that hide his name ;
It is so very long since last we came
The flowers we planted have had time to fade.

Nay, never plant fresh lilies, and renew
No roses ruined of the wind and rain ;
It may be long before we come again,
And these fresh flowers would then be faded
  too !

III.

I WILL not think the last farewell we hear
Is more than brief good-bye that a friend saith
Turning towards home that to our home lies
    near ;
I will not think so harshly of kind Death.

I will not think the last looks of dear eyes
Fade for the light that fades of our dim air,
But that the apparent glories of the skies
Weigh down their lids with beams too bright to
    bear.

Our dead have left us for no dark strange lands,
Unwelcomed there, and with no friends to meet—
But hands of angels hold the trembling hands,
And hands of angels guide the faltering feet.

I will not think the soul gropes dumb and blind
A brief space through our world, death-doomed
    from birth ;
I will not think that Love shall never find
A fairer heaven than he made of earth.

IV.

My dreams saw Death in no grim guise,
But with sweet words, and lips that smiled,
And gentle hands, and in his eyes
The meek looks of a little child.

Death had no shining sword to smite,
No crown of darkness on his head ;
Love took his hand without affright,
And followed smiling where he led.

V.

BY thine own soul's law learn to live,
And if men thwart thee, take no heed,
And if men hate thee, have no care,
But sing thy song, and do thy deed,
And hope thy hope, and pray thy prayer,
And claim no crown they will not give,
Nor bays they grudge thee for thy hair.

Keep thou thy soul-sworn steadfast oath,
And to thy heart be true thy heart,
What thy soul teaches learn to know,
And play out thine appointed part,
And thou shalt reap as thou shalt sow,
Nor helped nor hindered in thy growth
To thy full stature thou shalt grow.

Fix on the future's goal thy face,
And let thy feet be lured to stray

No whither, but be swift to run,
And nowhere tarry by the way,
Until at last the goal is won,
And thou may'st look back from thy place
And see thy long day's journey done.

VI.

So little time to speak, so much to say
        Without reply !
The day's work is to do, Lord, but the day
        Too soon will die !

Before the fight to fall out of the ranks,
        Dead and unslain !
To miss their glorious guerdon of God's thanks
        That die for men !

To fade before the sunset, when the noon
        Brightens my brow !—
Hush ! rebel heart, nor answer thou " Too soon,"
        When God calls " Now."

Whoso has loved the light, for him the sun
        Will rise anew !
Whoso has done his best leaves naught undone
        That man can do !

              In Manus Tuas, Domine !

SONGS OF THE SEA.

SONGS OF THE SEA.

I.

THE WRECK OF THE BIRKENHEAD.

TO THE MEMORY OF MY GRANDFATHER'S
FRIEND, THE WRONGED AND HEROIC
LORD DUNDONALD.

I.

THOU art mighty, O our mother, fair and strong,
All thy splendid names more splendid made by
 song,
Proclaim thy glory as thine empire wide !
For the poet has the hero for his brother,
And Shakespeare had not sung if Sidney had
 not died ;
Let thy foemen then revile thee how they will,
We, thy sons who love thee, know thee, mother,
The poet's and the hero's England still !

II.

O our mother, thine own sea
Saw never such a day for thee !
Not that memorable day
When that mighty Navy bore
Towards thine inviolable shore
The hate of Spain to spoil and slay,
And God blew with His winds, and where are
    they?
Flouted of thy proud sea's scorn,
Bruised and broken ere the morn,
Lay all their strength, as impotent a thing,
As the priest's curse and boasting of the King !
Nor that glad day whose light
Shone over the fair fight
At Navarino, nor that fatal day
That in Trafalgar's bay
Had Nelson's death to be remembered by,
O mother, as that whose sun saw these men die !

III.

On the deck of the sinking ship they stood
Together, rank set with rank, and arrayed
Not against their fellows for shedding of blood,
To die, not to kill, and the music played

To the colours flying on high, as they flew
Over Talavera and Waterloo !
" Ready "—the brave reply was a prayer ;
" Ready "—the heart of England spoke there,
Strong to command because strong to obey ;
" Ready "— to follow when Death led the way ;
" Ready "—to wait until Death drew near ;
" Ready "—their answer for Death to hear !

IV.

And they sent the boats away with a cheer,
And then closed in, file by file, to die—
And Death crept stealthily, plank by plank,
As though afraid, toward these without fear
Who waited his coming, till rank by rank,
Shoulder to shoulder, each comrade sank !

V.

And a swift wind caught up the bitter cry
From the heart of the shamed and remorseful
        sea,
And bore it to England, to bid her mourn
For her gallant dead that would never return,
And her grief grow glad for a great deed done,
And a famous day for her annals won !

VI.

O sleep sound beneath the waves, you, the record
of whose story
Shall fill the purest page of all our noble
England's glory !
Sleep, with England's sea for grave, O you
whose names shall be
One name with all the famous names remem-
bered of the sea !
Sleep, with this for epitaph : You were just such
Englishmen
As England at her need shall find ten thousand
such again !
As your fathers were, you were, and your sons
shall be like you,
And such deeds a simple duty for Englishmen
to do !

II.

OUR LADY OF ROSES.

WE knelt together at her shrine,
  Our Lady of The Flowers—
My true love's heart was sad as mine,
  And none so sad as ours !

He turned his head, and kissed me there,
  And vowed he loved me best—
And took the red rose from my hair,
  The white rose from my breast.

Before our Lady's golden throne,
  Our Lady of the Sea,
Where we two knelt I kneel alone,
  And pray for him and me.

Were he beside me at her shrine,
  Our Lady of the Flowers—

C

No heart as sorrowful as mine,
    Would grow as glad as ours.

But one night, as I lie asleep,
    My love will call to me :
"Love, ferry me across the deep
    Of Death's dream-beaconed sea."

And I shall take the oars and row
    Into the silent west,
Past cities sunken long ago
    Beneath the still sea's breast;

And hear the death-bells for the dead
    Toll from their shadowy spires,
And see the grey gulfs glowing red
    With flames of funeral fires !

Then will our Lady stretch her hand—
    Our Lady of the Sea—
And draw us safe to that fair strand
    Where all true hearts would be.

And we will kneel before her shrine,
    Our Lady of the Flowers,
And each maid's heart will be as mine,
    And all true hearts as ours !

III.

THE WITCH.

"A FAIR wind, and a swift sure wind
To bear your ship safe o'er the foam,
The wind that brings the sailor home,
And makes the rude sea smooth and kind,
  Who'll buy a wind of me?"

Thus sang a witch in Norroway,
A white witch fairer than the sea!

I said: "The land is far away
  Where my heart fain would be;
Sweet eyes grow dim for my delay,
And sweet lips paler when they pray,
And a true heart sadder every day—
  I'll buy a wind of thee."

"A fair wind, and a swift sure wind,
  The fair wind of the south,

Will I give thee, if thou giv'st me
One kiss of thy dear mouth."

" I will not buy thy wind of the south,
Nor any wind of thee;
I keep my kiss for her dear mouth
That prays at home for me."

"Then go thy way, thou'lt rue the day
Thou hadst such scorn of me,
And long thy love shall weep and pray
Ere thou come home from sea.
O fierce wind, and O swift wind born
The lord of the wild sea,
Be thy breath bitter as the scorn
Of his proud heart towards me!

"O fierce wind, be thy will to slay
As my heart's will in me—
I give the ship to be thy prey,
That bears him o'er the sea !"

" I do not fear thy hate, nor care
Though thy spells rule the sea,
Since than thy curse my true love's prayer
Shall more avail for me !}

"And though thy wind be fierce to slay,
   And fierce thy ravening sea,
God's peace shall be upon my way
   To where my heart would be,
And not in vain my love shall pray
   For her true love at sea!"

IV.

THE WITCH'S TRAGEDY.

The Witch is brought of The Abbot and The Friars of Mercy unto the beach of the sea, and there bound to a stake. Then The Abbot lifteth up the Cross, and saith unto the people:

WE give this sinner to the sea,
That its waves may wash her white and clean !

Then chant The Friars of Mercy:
Miserere, Domine !

A woman saith:
How young she is, and sweet and fair,
And hath our Guendolen's own hair !
Dear heart, I cannot see her die,
For our dead daughter's sake !

Her husband answereth:
Nor I,
Let us go hence.

A girl saith to her lover:
Is she so fair
That you must turn your eyes away?

Her lover answereth:
Be not so harsh, sweet !   Let us pray
For her that hath such need of prayer !

The girl saith:
Is your heart, too, caught in her snare?
Then is your heart no heart for me !

Then saith the Abbot:
We give this sinner to the sea,
That its waves may wash her white and clean !

Then chant The Friars of Mercy:
Miserere, Domine !

Then continueth The Abbot:
For Satan's leman she hath been !
His lust hath known her tender youth,
And kissed her on her maiden mouth !
Yea, sleeping by her mother's side
Her dreams would be defiled all night
With thoughts of their unclean delight,

And with hot words her longing cried
Upon her love, and without shame
She called him by his secret name
That rendered her for her lewd love—
The wicked wage and price thereof—
The malice of the evil eye ;
So that hale folk grow sick and die,
If she look on them, and the corn
Is blasted, and the babe unborn
Stifled within the mother's womb—
For which foul sin of hers her doom
Hath given this sinner to the sea !

Then chant The Friars of Mercy :
Miserere, Domine !

Then continueth The Abbot :
Lo, the sea riseth wave by wave,
And reacheth almost to her breast !
Where is her lover, where is he
That shall deliver her from the sea ?
Hath not his love strength left to save
Her tender body his lust knew ?
Shall no wave bear him on its crest ?
Shall not his dark wings cleave the air,
Nor earth gape wide and let him through ?

What keeps his help from her despair
That sees but Death upon the sea?

Then chant The Friars of Mercy :
Miserere, Domine !

A soldier saith :
This faith is no true soldier's faith
That makes such martyrs :
By His Death
That took our sins on Him and died,
And the Seven Wounds in His side,
I'd rather be a pagan Turk
Than have hand in such damned monks' work !

*Then saith The Witch, in a voice exceeding
sweet and clear :*
Jesu ! my Jesu ! I look for thee !
With the strength of Thy Love my heart is
stayed
Till thy feet walk over the waves of the sea !
Shall not the depths of the waters divide,
Nor let The Bridegroom's Love from the bride,
O Heavenly Bridegroom, Thy Love from me?
Hast Thou not heard, Lord, have I not prayed?
Shall the malice of men make my soul afraid?

Is Life too sweet to give up for Thy sake,
Too bitter Death to endure for Thy Love?
The life Thou gavest, the life these take
In the name of Thy Mercy, I lay this down,
This life, and in recompense thereof
Have the palm, and the amaranthine crown !

This is the sea of chrysopras
Seen in a vision by John of old,
Whose waves, over which His feet shall pass,
Shall shine with the light of His garment's gold,
His wedding garment's put on for me !
Sure of His promise, safe in His love,
O sea, I feel thy waves at my breast
That bring me my Bridegroom at last, O sea !
Jesu, my soul hath the wings of a dove,
And flieth away and is at rest.

*Then the waves close over her. Afterwards
cometh this marvel to pass: the waters of the
sea divide, and through the glory of them
flieth a dove.*

V.

SUNRISE AT SEA.

You hardly live, what should you know of Death?
Your shallows scarcely feel the morning's fire,
Meek streams, how should you hear what my
     soul saith,
Or know the passion of my heart's desire?

Let finch and linnet sing you on your way,
And winds that talk with quiet fields and trees—
My soul would know what morning's has to say,
And hear the sun's heart speaking with the sea's

SONGS OF THE STREETS.

SONGS OF THE STREETS.

I.

THE LAST BARRICADE OF THE COMMUNE.

AT the dark close of that disastrous day
Whose sun went redder with our blood to God,
When the last few were shot whom Gallifet
Had picked for death, and Mannikin-Metter-
    nich [1]
Might glut his little soul to see the broad
Deserted streets strewn with dead bodies thick,
His butchers, wearied of their work at length,
Halted from plying of their bloody trade
To curse the Prussians or the Emperor,
And laughed and joked ('tis a good jest to kill
Men without arms and women without strength,

[1] Thiers.

Since there is no risk to spoil the sport !) and
    swore
Sullenly that no more blood was to spill ;
Then marched ; but when they reached the
    barricade
We had abandoned last, a little head
Lifted its golden curls, and a child said :
"Vive la Commune !"—and then stood still and
    smiled,
Folding his little arms across his breast—
Until one beast, more beast-like than the rest
Suddenly raised his gun and shot the child !

II.

THE CHILDREN'S PLAYGROUND.

POOR little children, this place of death
  Is your only place for play !
Here only you feel the warm wind's breath
  That tells shut buds of May !

You touch the marble, smell to the flowers,
  Till the eldest child will say :
" We can never have such graves for ours,
  So pretty—for one must pay,

" And pretty things cost so much to buy,
  And are not given, but sold ;
Our graves are like our beds when we die,
  Our beds where we sob with cold ! "

Poor little children, His sheep unfed,
  How little of earth is given,
Of His earth to you of whom He said :
  " Of such is the Kingdom of Heaven ! "

D

III.

SELLING FLOWERS.

POOR child, your brown hands offer me
These flowers that only mean for you
So many pence—this rose that tells
No story of warm skies and blue,
And happy hills and pleasant dells,
And woods your eyes will never see.

Sometimes a little child like you,
Holding his mother's hand, will show
Your flowers with eager looks, and talk
Of fresher flowers that used to grow
In those green fields that once they knew
So sweet to play in and to walk,
Before they came to the dark town.

And sometimes, pacing up and down,
Some wretched weary woman, gay

With hideous merriment, will hush
Her laugh, and with a startled blush
Turn round and look another way.
But all these have no pence to spare,
Let such pass on, and long, and stare.

Poor child, here are the pence you lack,
And, here, I give you your flowers back,
To talk with, play with, love ; these are
Your own, and you will promise me
You will not sell nor throw away
Your flowers, but keep them, though they be
Faded and without scent—while they
Are with you God will not be far.

IV.

A REJECTED ROSE.

As I toiled in my dreary room,
So wretched, and dull, and high
To be nearer the dismal sky,
I threw my rose in the street,
For I saw its leaves in the glass
Beginning to droop and die—
Then I watched the people pass
Like ghosts through the dense fog's gloom,
Till a girl from among the rest
That hurried unheeding by
Picked up my rose at her feet
With a sudden eager cry,
And sheltered its leaves in her breast.

My rose that I threw away,
A despised and rejected thing,
To her my rose meant May,
And woods where glad birds sing,

And June, and the longest day,
And all that lovers say
For only the spring to hear !
And the skies of the sorrowful city
Grew suddenly bright and clear,
And smiled with God's own pity !

Poor girl, with your eager eyes,
Innocent sister and wise,
Your heart knows more than we
Of all things gracious and sweet !
For we watch through our prison-bars
To vex the unanswering stars
With question of what shall be,
And have no eyes to see
The blossoms at our feet—
And an Ariel in each tree
Waits our spells to set him free,
But the charms of Prospero
Were forgotten long ago.
And so, when the day is done,
And its burden and heat overpast,
Unreluctant and undismayed
We fall upon sleep at last
In the darkness that maketh afraid,

Having never seen the sun
Shine on the world God made !—

My sister, unknown and dear,
One day I shall see you stand
On the steps of The Golden Stair
With my rose in your golden hair,
And you will take my hand,
And I shall feel no fear.

V.

QUIA MULTUM AMAVIT.

HUSH, dearest, the milk in my breast is dry,
> There's none for you—
Would the blood in my heart that hears your
> cry
>> Were too !

Hush, my own ! Children close their eyes at
> night
>> When mothers weep,
And light from their heaven of dreams makes
> bright
>> Their sleep.

Hush, sweet ! Want and sorrow have said their
> say,
>> And wrought their will—
Hush, dear ! we have done with the weary day,
>> Sleep still !

Hush, *his* own! Though your mother's eyes are
  dim,
    Your father's bride
Must have her dress when to-morrow with him
    Beside

She kneels before God for the world to see
    And in His name
Call holy and bless the love that in me
    Was shame!

You are sleeping now, you will cry no more—
    Sleep, till the light!
Sleep, sweet! I must sew, though my eyes are
  sore,
    All night.

Asleep, at last! when I kissed you, you smiled
    And turned your head
To kiss me! Asleep, dear? O God, my child
    Is dead!

SONGS OF SALUTATION.

SONGS OF SALUTATION.

I.

A DEDICATION: TO RICHARD HENGIST HORNE.

MASTER, beloved for memory
Of all high hearts that held thee dear,
I bring my gifts for thee to see,
I sing my songs for thee to hear,
And at thy Muse's shrine lay down
The buds I gathered for her crown.

Dear Master, take what gifts are ours,
And let thy brows scorn not to wear
The garland of what fading flowers
Our mortal summer finds most fair,
Till our sun miss thee, and thou be
Where Marlowe's spirit waits for thee.

II.

TO MICHAEL FIELD.

THE Lesbian sea gives up her dead,
  And on her gleaming wave
Each borne from her green bed
The gold-haired Nereids throng
To hear their risen Sappho's song
  Round her Leucadian grave.

Sappho, what strange and subtle speech
  Did the cold secret sea
That bore thy goddess teach
Thy lips, what wild sweet thing
Have the waves taught thy heart to sing
  Unknown on earth to thee?

What has the silence told thy sleep
  More passionate and dear?

What songs more sweet and deep
Than in thy Lesbian sky
The sunset's heart heard, loth to die,
  And slain with joy to hear.

Ah, who may hear thy song aright
  That none may dare to praise?
Forlorn of bloom and light
Our lives may never know
The skies and songs of Long Ago
  In these doom-darkened days!

III.

A GARLAND: TO ARTHUR
O'SHAUGHNESSY.

WHAT chill sad blossoms of our northern air
Shall my hands gather and your heart find fair?
What pale buds grown beneath our sun's cold
        beams
Might make a garland for your Muse's hair?

Seeing how before her tender rapt eyes gleams
That unforgotten country of her dreams,[1]
And glowing secret of that far-off land,
Songs of dead birds and murmurs of lost streams,

And holier memories of that gracious band
Whose smile the dull world might not under-
        stand

[1] " Nostalgie des Cieux."

That were her glorious kinsfolk, and content
Of happy lovers wandering hand in hand.

How in this dark place of her banishment
Shall she forget the joyous days she spent
In that remembered country? Shall she stay
Among us, and no thought be thither sent?

And often at the closing of our day
Will she not fain take ship and leave our May,
And sail beyond the limit of our skies
Towards Erumango lying far away?[1]

Nay, but our grief pleads with her memories,
And she forgoes the joy our life denies,
And deep delight whereof her soul is fain,
And human tears have made more sweet her eyes.

She leaves her fair far heaven to dwell with
      men,
And seeing them so dull and full of pain
She softly asks of God to comfort these
With tender lips that sing Christ back again,[2]

---

[1] "Azure Islands."   [2] "Christ will Return."

To bring Love with Him, Hope and Joy and
    Peace,
That Want and Wrong and Sin and Shame may
    cease,
And evil things and sorrowful take flight
And leave our changed world lovely—and she
    sees

Amid the heavy horror of the night
The splendour of our sunrise, and the might
Of one United Europe fair and free,[1]
And all the morning's music and the light.

And I that watch until that glad time be
That God has given her pure eyes grace to see,
And looking towards the dim East find no sign,
Within your Muse's temple reverently,

Brother, I come, but seeing her so divine,
I dare not offer what poor gifts are mine,
And worship with bowed head and bended knee,
And pass, and lay no garland on her shrine.

[1] " Europe."

IV.

TO A MUSICIAN.

YOU hear the pulses of Beethoven's heart,
Or walk with Weber in a place ghoul-haunted,
Or wander, by some gentle spell enchanted,
In some melodious dreamland of Mozart ;
To you the comfort of your gracious art
Gives all things beautiful, the sighing seas,
The murmuring winds, the woodland-wandering
      bees,
And singing birds of your delight are part !

In every wood your soul the Dryad hears,
And on the hillsides the forsaken Pan,
But me the discord of the clamorous years
Will not let live with nature, but with man
I dwell, O friend, and of his hopes and fears
Make me as sweet a music as I can.

E

SONGS OF LOVE AND DEATH.

SONGS OF LOVE AND DEATH.

I.

THE SCULPTOR.

ONLY a month, and she weds the King !
Only a month, and my statue stands
With a crowd of courtiers either side
That stare and simper my praise whose hands
Have wrought the bridegroom his marble bride
With meek eyes blessing the world like Spring !

With meek eyes blessing the world unknown,
And heart the wings of a golden dove
Bear to that land of enchantment sweet
Where she walks with rosy skies above
Over the roses under her feet,
A great queen crowned, to her royal throne !

Only a month, and I steal apart
From the fools that gape at my work and me
To the room where my waxen bride gleams
    white,
For only the moon and my soul to see
The form I wrought with the help of night,
That smiles—with a pin's prick in her heart !

II.

MAY MARGARET.

MAY MARGARET has no will to walk
   Within the garden-close;
She passeth the white lilies by,
   And leaveth the white rose.

" Tell me truly, daughter dear,
   As I lay awake last night
What was the sound that I did hear ? "
   "Some sad ghost sighing at the light,

Or wind, or falling of the rain "—
   "Nay daughter, of all these that was none "—
" O mother, it was my moaning you heard
   To bear a little son !

" I took him to the forest dim
   Ere men should wake to see,

And there in a grave I buried him,
And there you'll bury me,
Dear mother, and leave space for one
Will soon come to make three ! "

III.

JAFFEER, THE BARMECIDE.

Said the mighty Caliph Haroun to Jaffeer the
    Barmecide:

"In such honour do we hold thee, O Jaffeer,
    that for bride

We bestow on thee our sister, but on peril of
    thy life

Do not thou presume to love her whom we give
    thee for a wife!

By the beard of the Prophet, if she have of thee
    a child,

If within her veins our royal blood with thine
    should be defiled,

Be thou sure the bow-string waits thee, and the
    sack awaits the bride"—

" Lord, to hear is to obey thee," said Jaffeer the
    Barmecide.

So between these at their bridal Fear stood
    frowning, but above

Love smiled on these lovers wedded and com-
    manded not to love,
And she knew her husband's footfall at her
    chamber-door, and night
Kept inviolate these lovers and their secret of
    delight.

And secret days, and weeks, and months, in
    forbidden joy were past,
Till Love grew too strong for cunning, and
    betrayed them at the last.

And at midnight to the chamber where these
    lovers dreamed and slept
Followed of his mutes and headsmen still as
    Fear Haroun crept,
And his mutes there strangled her ere her lips
    could cry a word ;
But the Caliph looked on Jaffeer for a space,
    then drew his sword,
Then the blade flashed through the darkness, on
    the floor the shorn head rolled ;
And he signed his headsman to him : "Cram
    these slaves' throats full of gold
Till they choke—what I command thee see
    thou straightway that be done—

Also send my women hither, for I would not
 be alone,
And my jester—I am heavy at my heart now,
 and have need
Of his wit to make me laughter—though, by
 Allah, of this deed
I repent not when I think on all their shameful
 sin forbid,
I remember how I loved them," said the Caliph
 Alraschid.

IV.

PALOMEDES.

I SURELY think that I shall win to-day,
Yea, and my heart is well assured of it,
With God to help—since, last night, as I lay
Asleep, with some sweet vision of my sweet

Held fast between mine eyelids, the close night
Brake as a bud unfolding into bloom,
Until mine eyes were startled with the light
Of a great glory filling all my room,

And in the shining of that hallowed air
The brightness of three angels gleamed around
Radiantly; and in their hands they bare
Bright arms, which on my body having bound,

They set a shining sword into my hand,
And then the splendour vanished from the place,

And I woke, clutching vainly at the brand,
And felt the morning strike upon my face.

So have I a sure hope I shall prevail
To-day, and my poor strength be found above
The strength of Launcelot—yea, how should I
    fail
That have so sweet a lady for my love?

V.

BICE.

I HAD a vision of fair ladies dead
That song keeps living for us, and makes fair
The faded faces and discoloured hair,
And sets a garland,on each fallen head,
And Love confirms their immortality
So that their gentle presence still is nigh
All lovers, and the pulse of their dead bliss
Passionately unforgotten in the kiss
Of clinging lips, and warmth of claspèd hands,
And there is no true heart but understands
The sweetness of their story—and with these
    came
When folk were met upon a holiday
To welcome in the sweetness of the May
With laughter, and fair pastime, and glad game,
A little maid with grave and gentle eyes

Sweet as vague looks of dawn-awakened birds,
And red mouth fashioned for all gracious words;
And next her stood a little lad apart
From all his happy fellows at their play,
And did forget the sweetness of the May,
And did forget the folk at holiday,
But felt the great love growing at his heart,
And the beginning of that New Life sweet
That makes the whole world musical with it
Until all song cease, and continually
Would look on her with fate-acquainted eyes
That knew then first how they should after see
Hell, Purgatory, and Paradise.

VI.

EVE.

WHY art thou sad, love, for the loss of Eden?
Let us go hence together side by side,
Thou Man, dear, and I Woman and thy Bride!
Too long we two dwelt there—slaves, scared and
    chidden,
Before I, Eve, ate of the fruit forbidden,
And having tasted thereof gave to thee,
My husband, and thy soul as mine grew free,
And good and evil were no longer hidden

From our eyes purged of darkness to discern
The knowledge that God feared lest we should
    learn
And no more worship Him nor call Him Lord—
Let us go hence, love, masters of our fate,
Past His armed angel standing by the gate,
Nor fear the menace of the flaming sword!

VII.

AT LOVE'S GRAVE.

WE sought the grave in the shadow and gloom
  Where we laid our Love when he died—
An angel stood beside the tomb,
  And the doors were open wide.

" Whence do you come, and who are ye,
  And whom seek you here," he said :
" Mourners," we answered him, " are we
  That come to look on our dead.

" Forbid us not, we are weary now
  That have travelled far and wide
To see the wounds of the thorns on His brow
  And the cruel nails in His side."

" Go hence," he said, " that refused Him aid
  And left your Lord to die,
Recreant hearts, that ashamed and afraid
  Kept far when His foes were nigh.

F

" For all the passion of all the pain
  With which your weak hearts grieve,
If Love should come on earth again
  Again would you not believe,

" Again deny Him, betray once more,
  Again be stubborn in sin "—
We knelt beside the open door
  And dared not enter in.

VIII.

THE DEATH OF HAMPDEN.

A tent in the Parliamentary camp. HAMPDEN
lies wounded, and CROMWELL *is bending over*
him.

HAMPDEN.

SPARE all who yield ! Alas, that we must pierce
One English heart for England !—I thank you,
    sir,
My wound is nothing ; a little loss of blood ;
I fear much more must flow from worthier veins
Ere England's hurt be healed.

CROMWELL.

Alas ! how strong are base things to destroy !
The brute's part in them kills the god's in us,
And robs the world of many glorious deeds—
In all the histories of famous men
We never find the greatest overthrown

Of their high equals, but the loftiest head,
Screened of its laurels from the lightning's flash,
Falls by some chance blow of an obscure hand,
And glory cannot guard the hero's heart
Against the least knave's dagger.

HAMPDEN.

You cannot help me—
Save yourself, sir ; my best prayers keep you
    safe—
I fain would win as far as yonder house ;
It was my dead dear wife's ; such shapes are
    there
As I would see about my dying bed
To make me sure of heaven.—Forgive me, love,
That I am loth to come yet to thy heart;
I have only lived without thee, O my best,
That I might live for England.—
                    Is Cromwell come ?

CROMWELL.

How is it with you, cousin ?

HAMPDEN.

Very well;
With hope to be soon better ; gentle cousin,

I have scant time to speak, and much to say
That thou must hear.   Men's eyes more clearly
    see
Ere the long darkness ; and thus plagues, and
    wars,
Earthquake, and overthrow of prosperous states
Have been foretold by lips of dying men :—
But I die happy, with a joy too keen
For this weak wounded body, and delight
Of eager youth that dreams of noble deeds,
Knowing the greatness in thee, which occasion
Has not yet shown the world, and thine own
    self
Hast only dimly guessed at.—These hands I
    hold
Shall bear the weight of England's greatness up ;
Thy name, mine own dear kinsman's, shall have
    sound
More royal than all crownèd kings' ; the slave
Shall murmur it in dreams of liberty,
The patriot in his dungeon, and endure,
The tyrant, and grow merciful for fear ;
And when thou hast done high and song-worthy
    deeds
At length shall come thy poet, whose purer eyes
God shall seclude from sight of our gross earth,

And for the dull light of our darker day
Give all heaven to his vision, star with star
Shining, and splendid, and and sonorous spheres
To make him music, and those sacred lips,
More eloquent than the Mantuan's, praising thee,
Shall make thy name a memory for all time,
And set a loftier laurel on thy head
Than any gathered from red fields of war ;
So great shall England's great need make thee,
      Cromwell ;
Whom thou forget not still to love and serve,
Holding thy greatness given to make her great,
Thy strength to keep her strong— then (since
      Oblivion
Is what men chiefly fear in death) dear cousin
I would not be forgotten of thy love.
And now I am loth the last words I shall speak
Must be of strife—yet I must utter them :—
Be not of those that vex the angry times
With meek-mouthed proffers of rejected peace ;
When men have set the justice of their cause
To sharp arbitrament of answering arms,
Tongues should keep mute, and steel hold speech
      with steel,
Till victory can plead the conquered's cause,
And make soft mercy no more dangerous ;

We must o'ercome our foes to make them
　　friends.
Thy hand, dear cousin.　Sweet, I hear thy voice
That calls me, and leave England for thy sake—
Kiss me, dear love, and take my soul to God !
—Receive my soul, Lord Jesus!—O God, save
My country.—God be merciful to——

CROMWELL.

O Lord of Hosts, if Thou wilt only give me
An England with but three such Englishmen,
My life shall be as noble as this man's.
Farewell, dear cousin, perfect heart that beats
No more for England.　Think of me in Heaven,
And help to make me all thou saidst I should be !

(*Kneels down by the bed.　Rising and looking
　　steadfastly on the dead face of* HAMPDEN,)

Yea, and I shall be.

IX.

ST. CATHERINE OF SIENA.

*A street in Siena.   A scaffold, and a crowd
about it.*

FIRST CITIZEN.
When should he come?

SECOND CITIZEN.
                        It wants yet some half-hour ;
Does your impatience grudge him so much life?

A WOMAN.
They say the man will die a penitent,
One hopeful of God's grace and reconciled
To human justice, and this change in him
Was wrought by sweet persuasion of that lady
Famed for her life of gracious charities,
Catherine, who will walk with him to his death,
So he hath asked her.

SECOND CITIZEN.

She is a noble lady,
A virgin vowed and dedicate to God;
Her common words are holier than our prayers,
And if she pass them walking in the street
Men seem to see a glory on her hair,
And in her eyes the look of one that hears
The inexpressive melodies of heaven,
And the changed place grow radiant with the
    light
Flashed from the splendour of an angel's wings.
And when the dark days come upon this land,
When this dear nursling, this fair child of Time,
Held fast of Freedom to her breasts of love,
This promise-pledge of Hope, this Italy
Shall share the fate of all things beautiful,
And her sons die to free her and leave her
    bound,
When the fierce Austrian eagle gapes for prey,
And darkens with the horror of his wings
This else unshadowed heaven, God shall send
A second Christ of a more holy faith,[1]
And he shall touch men's blind eyes sealed in
    sleep,

[1] Joseph Mazzini.

And let in the true dawn on their false dreams,
Then Rome shall be more great than all her
    past,
And her imperial bridegroom wed again
.Venice, and Florence be more beautiful
Than all her flowers that give her that sweet
    name ;
This shall God do for this sweet lady's sake.

FIRST CITIZEN.

Do you not hear the cry that brings him hither?
The men-at-arms march first, and in their midst
He walks with bounden hands, and looks towards
    her
With childlike-trustful and obedient eyes:
And now they halt ; and now she speaks with
    him ;
And he kneels down as though in prayer.

A WOMAN.

                                        Ah, God !
How the great axe takes colour from the sun !
I dare no longer look.

  [*The executioner strikes, and the man's head
    falls.* CATHERINE *lifts it in her hands, and
    comes forward as though to speak.*]

SECOND CITIZEN.

Silence, she would speak.

CATHERINE.

What words of mine should touch you, if this
    sight
Have left your hearts unmoved, if these closed
    eyes
Fill not your eyes with tears, if these dumb lips
Plead not with you that none again may die
Such death as this man's—Christ is not your
    Christ,
But of poor folk, and sad, and heavy-laden,
And if you bring Him gifts of gold and myrrh,
Thank-offerings of your riches, and cry : "Lord,
I have lived my life according to thy law,
Shunning the ways of sinners, and all these
For thy love-sake have hated," Christ will answer :
"Are there none such to plead against my wrath,
No sinner to pray for thee—fool, hast thou
None whom all men have hated that hath loved
    thee?"
O sirs, you should have anger against the sin,
But pity for the sinner, and not thrust
A violent life out of your violent world
With cursing, but should rather think how much

You have and need to make yours different—
A guarded youth of love-protected years,
And little tender trivial things, small wants
And sweet that make your life sweet ; but these
    have lost
The passionate rebellion of the heart
That tells us we were made for happiness,
And fall into a sullen discontent
Enduring sufferings of the beasts that make
Men beast-like, cold and hunger, curses and
    blows ;
Sirs, if you miss some dead face, look for one
Forlorn and sorrowful to fill your heart,
And speak sweet words you shall not hear again
From dumb dear lips to these that never heard ;
And would you surely find Love, search for him
Where God doth chiefly seek him, in sad hearts
Their sorrow teaches to hold precious
The unfamiliar music of His name ;
Sirs, if sad eyes grow glad because of you,
Your own shall weep no more, and if harsh lips
Speak softly for your sake, yours shall not sigh,
For our good deeds are our best comforters.
O sirs, you know I speak not of myself
Vain words, but these my Christ has bidden me
    say—

My Christ, Whose bride am I espoused in faith—
For at the time when all the world holds feast,
Withdrawing from its foolish revelry,
I knelt in prayer, and falling in a swoon
Heard a strange music, wonderful and sweet,
A mingling of all sounds in one sweet tune,
As though all April sang with one bird's voice ;
And then a sudden splendour filled the room,
And from the glory came a voice that said :
" My sister, my belovèd, I am come
According to my promise," and my Christ
Stood face to face with me, and at His side
The Holy Mother, and the Evangelist
John, and the Apostle Paul, and Dominic,
And with these David playing on a harp ;
And then the Holy Mother took my hand
And led me to the Son, who placed on it
A golden ring set with four precious stones ;—
And since I went among poor folk, and wrought
With simple sweet sufficiency of service
My Lord's appointed work—until I heard
Of one that lay in bonds and doomed to death,
And coming to his prison found this man
Silent, with sullen and resentful eyes ;
Then I knelt down beside him, and took the hand
That had shed so much blood, and talked with him

Of divine love and human brotherhood
Until his heart was softened and he wept ;
And so he came a penitent to death.—
O sirs, I charge all you that saw him die,
Pray that this man may pray for you to-night
For he shall be with Christ in Paradise ;
In sign whereof I kiss him on his face.

X.

THE DEATH OF MARCIA.

Michael Stolskoi's cell.

MICHAEL STOLSKOI.

THIS is the last night of my nights on earth.
Bright moon, how often have I seen thy face
Look on me past some continent of cloud !
How often have I seen thee with bright beams
Holding the quarry of the night in chase,
And all thy starry sisters in thy train ;
How often hast thou kissed me in my sleep,
As though I were Endymion and thy love !
Tired Sleep clings close to Night, and holds her
      fast
For fear of evil dreams, and Night looks down
On all the unquiet sorrows of the world,
And beckons Death with an uplifted hand.
We shall be friends to-morrow, Death and I ;
Youth never met him in his wanderings,
And never talked with Death, but only saw

Some phantom glide between him and the sun
Sighing, and passed on with hands full of flowers,
And April on his lips and in his eyes.
What will you shew me, Death, that I would see,
What will you tell me, Death, that I would hear?
What secrets that the wisest have not learnt ?
Dread King, mine eyes shall meet thine unafraid,
My hand not tremble at the touch of thine ;
My voice shall fail not when I hear thee speak,
Nor my feet falter as they follow thee—
I am glad I shall die young, ere Love has seen
The few I love grow fewer from year to year,—
The hand that held mine fast on Life's dark way,
The cheerful comrade of my wanderings,
That walked a few miles at my side, and showed
My path, and left me with a kind farewell
To end my journey on that lonely road
By which Death leads us to our rest, and find
Night with no moon nor any stars to guide,
And day with some blurred shadow of the sun—
I shall not drain life's chalice to the dregs,
But leave the feasters ere the feast is done,
Its music on my lips and in my ears !
Is not this better than to warm cold hands
Above the ashes of a lonely hearth ?
I shall not have outlived desire of life,

And seen all fair things laid in some deep grave
With some old sweet word for an epitaph,
Before my own is dug ; I shall not die
Only when all my joys are dead, but take
Some sweet regret of earth to make heaven
    fairer.
Love talks of those that died young with hushed
    voice
And tender tears, those whose stay with him
Was briefer than his visions of delight
Live longest in Love's faithful memory ;
Spring's flowers would be forgotten, if their bloom
Survived the fond last smile of May's farewell ;
We must die old to make remembrance pass
Beside our dust with careless feet and eyes,
And hands that have no garland for our graves
All gracious things die young, Love, Hope, and
    Faith,
Sweet Hope, the illusion of the soul, and Love,
The illusion of the heart, and Faith that dreams
Of brighter worlds, and sees our sun and stars
Shadows across the splendour of her dreams.
Only hard hearts live long in this hard world !
The proud, the noble, and the indignant break,
As the sun dies before the dark night comes
And leaves the world made hateful by her reign.

"Those the Gods love die young ;" the Gods
    are wise
That take their favourites to themselves again
Ere those they love forget them or forsake ;
Apollo, had he with Admetus passed
Some few more years of exile, had remembered
No more Olympus, and that harmony
Earth could no longer keep nor the Gods lack
Had grown as common as dull shepherds' songs
That told the woods of Amaryllis' scorn ;
Had the fates spared Marcellus, he had died,
Like the first Cæsar, by some Brutus' hand,
After ambition made his fame forget
Laurels, not gold, should crown a hero's head ;
And Nero, had he died young, might have been
Mourned like Marcellus, with such golden tears
As melt men's hearts that read of Virgil's grief.
We fear too much our natural graves, too little
The daily graves that Life digs for our souls,
And covers over with false leaves and flowers.
Better that Youth met Death with steadfast
    looks,
With head uplifted, and untrembling hands,
And Beauty with her lustrous eyes undimmed,
Than that his malice triumphed o'er our fears,
O'er palsied limbs and undetermined hearts.

(*Enter* MARCIA *and the* GAOLER.)

MICHAEL STOLSKOI.

Marcia ! How came you hither, and who is this ?

GAOLER.

A friend.

MARCIA (*to the* GAOLER.)
Give me the pistol and the poison.
Here is more gold—had I thrice more to give
My thanks were still your debtors for this service.

GAOLER.

You have more than paid me both in gold and
thanks.
(*To* MICHAEL STOLSKOI.) I am the spy you
might have slain, but spared
To help you and this lady at your need—
Let me but touch your hand, and mine will feel
More like an honest man's.

MICHAEL STOLSKOI.
Here is my hand,
And with my heart I thank you.

GAOLER.
Farewell, sir—

And farewell, noble lady—God watch o'er you !

[*Exit* GAOLER.

MARCIA.

You will not scorn me now? You will be kind?
Death reconciles us with our enemies,
And I have loved you—God will tell you how—
How changed a woman I have been at heart
Since first I saw you, and my soul leapt forth
With a great cry toward you, as one that gropes
Out of the maze of some dark dream, and feels
The sudden sun strike on his eyes ; my past
Was as the hiss of waters in men's ears
That sink for the last time, and see some hand
Stretched out to save them.—Dearest, I have
          been dead,
And God has sent my spirit back to earth
To love thee as some saint or angel might ;
Give me your hands ; God will forgive me soon ;
And you will love me.

MICHAEL STOLSKOI.
                    I read within your heart
The story of your life, blotted with tears
Of penitence and shame that come of love—
If only love had found you, ere your own

Had learnt the teaching of those hateful hearts
That should have kept you pure and innocent
As when you came from heaven, but taught your
    youth
The shameful secrets of man's lust, and sold
Your beauty in the market for such wares,
Love had then told you how divine a thing
Is woman's beauty, terrible and fair
With light from Heaven or with fire from Hell.
Come close to mine, poor heart, and let me teach
    thee
How glad and good and pure thou might'st have
    been.
    [*Takes* MARCIA *in his arms and kisses her.*

MARCIA (*in* MICHAEL'S *arms, and looking up
into his eyes*).
Dear, since you love me, 'tis not hard to die !

MICHAEL STOLSKOI.
Not for your woman's heart, but hard for mine—
Men will not so soon sever from their joys,
And lack the meek submission of the will,
The patient fortitude that bows the head
And bares the breast to the descending stroke,
And resignation, that are woman's strength ;

We chafe against the masterdom of Fate,
Disputing the supremacy of Death
With proud defiant eyes as of strong lords
Over all other powers on earth but his.

MARCIA.

I do not grudge Death what poor joys he takes
Once having had more than Hope asked of Life,
The last look of your eyes, and your last thought,
The last beat of your heart before mine breaks
And Love's last kisses sweeter than the first.

MICHAEL STOLSKOI (*leading her to the window*).
Look yonder, love, how bright a world is there !
Fair world, I am loth to take farewell of you !

MARCIA.

How much more fair a Heaven ! Fair Heaven
        I am glad
My love and I shall find to-night in you
One of the many mansions of God's House !
Surely thy bright stars are true lovers' souls !
Dear, do not deem death is that dreaded thing
Of our weak fears and unjust surmise !
Have you forgotten your own song of Death,

How Life stood on a sudden face to face
With Death, and felt no fear, and sang to Death?

[*Sings.*

Sweet friend, I had not thought to see
　　Thy face so soon, or hear
Thy gentle voice that calls to me,
　　And bids me feel no fear;

Only one kiss, then let us go,
　　True lover, hand in hand,
Across the moors, across the snow,
　　Into the distant land.

O, guide me! lest my feet should stray,
　　And hush my heart on thine;
No sun is bright upon our way,
　　Nor moon nor star shall shine;

But we shall hear Cocytus roar
　　When all earth's streams are dumb,
And light-heeled Hermes goes before
　　To tell the dead we come.

Love will not think that world of night
　　A sadder world than ours;

But those dim skies have their own light,
And those dark fields their flowers !

Think not so sadly of death ; you would not
make
Death terrible to me ?

MICHAEL STOLSKOI.
O my own love !
I have another love plucks at my heart
And will not let it die content on thine,
But calls my eager spirit back to earth
From those bright thresholds of a heaven with
thee—
The love of our dear Poland.—O, my best,
Death has no bitterer anguish than to see
The invader's foot spurning the sacred earth
That holds the dear dust of our dead ; his arms
And flaunting banners of his triumph hung
Within the Temple of our fathers' fame ;
To see his soldiers strutting through our streets,
And patiently submit to the disdain
Of such ignoble conquerors.   O, to see
Our country's language, laws, and ancient customs
Abolished and forbidden, and her sons
Taught to renounce her in an alien tongue !

Better a thousand wars with all their woes,
And better that our land were one wide grave ;
Better the cry of Rachel for her children,
And better Rizpah's vigil by her dead
Than this sad, shameful motherhood of slaves
That live by sufferance of a tyrant's will.

MARCIA.

Be comforted, dear love, in God's good time
Our land shall find deliverance ; never country
Was long enslaved that had such hearts as thine !

MICHAEL STOLSKOI.

The few that loved our Poland yesterday
To-morrow will be fewer ! My faithful friends !
What land could spare such true hearts at her
    need ?

MARCIA.

Dear, do not die in this sad disbelief,
But hear Hope's heavenly message to our souls,
And sweet assurance of our granted prayers.
(*Kneeling.*) O Lord, remember Poland !—

MICHAEL STOLSKOI.

                        Lord, Amen !

MARCIA.

Amen ! See, love, the light comes at our prayer !
The winds of morning stir in the still east,
And night flies star by star before the sun.—
Let those that come with day not find us here—
Love, we must die—I first—by your dear hand ;
Here is the pistol !

MICHAEL STOLSKOI.

O ! I cannot do it !
Some other way but that !

[*Puts the pistol in his breast.*

MARCIA.

The poison then—
The queen that cast a pearl into her cup
Richer than tribute of a hundred isles
Pledged Antony in no such royal wise
As I my love.   One kiss before I drink !

[MICHAEL STOLSKOI *kisses her, and she
drinks.*

MICHAEL STOLSKOI.

Sweet, let me take death from your lips and hands !

[*Drinks.*

MARCIA (*dying*).

Is not this heaven I see ? And these are spirits
That sing so sweetly to their golden harps !
Dear love, I know the meaning of their song,
Because they sing of love—only of love—
Love, love—and Paradise for those that love—
No more the mere gross earth too poor for love !
[*Dies.*

MICHAEL STOLSKOI.

Sweet spirit, have no fear to stand alone
Among God's angels ! Wait, love, till I come,
I will not keep thee long !

[*The doors are thrown open.* THE TYRANT
enters, followed by THE EXECUTIONER *and
his assistants.* MICHAEL *rises and stands
between them and* MARCIA'S *dead body.*

THE EXECUTIONER.
                    We have him safe,
Your Majesty ; the gaoler's flight has left
His prisoner behind.

THE TYRANT (*seeing* MARCIA'S *dead body*).
                    Who is this woman ?

MICHAEL STOLSKOI.

Marcia—my love !

THE TYRANT.

Thy love? Insolent liar !

[*Strikes* MICHAEL STOLSKOI.

MICHAEL STOLSKOI.

Thou hast done thy last ill deed—Go down to
hell,

And ask thy wages of thy taskmaster!

[*Draws the pistol from his breast, and
shoots the* CZAR.

THE TYRANT (*falling into the arms of*
THE EXECUTIONER).

Help ! I am slain ! The torture for yon villain !

Do not forget the torture !

MICHAEL STOLSKOI (*falling on* MARCIA'S
body).

Death mocks thy hate !

[*The day breaks, and the sun throws its light
from the bars of the window on* MICHAEL
STOLSKOI, *and* MARCIA *clasped in his arms*

MICHAEL STOLSKOI (*lifting up his head*).
Light, light, more light, O God, for thy dark
world !

[*Falls back dead.*

LILIA.

"Manibus date Lilia plenis."

"Les morts sont morts, douce leur soit l'éternité."

PAUL VERLAINE.

LILIA.

I.

JEAN BAPTISTE VICTOR BAUDIN.

SHALL not we miss thee, brother, at our side,
And on our lips the high triumphal song
Be changed into a dirge for thee that died?
Nay, sorrow shall not do thy fame such wrong
To wish to have thee living, for such men
As thou must die when Liberty is slain.

Where honour was no more thou couldst not be,
And Fate, that had but shameful days to give,
Closed fast those noble eyes lest they should
    see
Liberty dead ere thou hadst ceased to live,
And, ere she gave France to her tyrant, gave
Thy sacred dust an unpolluted grave.

The praise of unheard lips, the reverence
Of unknown hearts, the tears of eyes unseen,
O brother, are not these a recompense
For life as noble as thy life had been?
And all these death has given thee, to keep
A loving watch beside thy sacred sleep.

II.

A FUNERAL WREATH.

IN MEMORY OF ARTHUR WILLIAM EDGAR O'SHAUGHNESSY.

THIS was no time for thee to pass away,
This dark, cold month, forlorn of light and
　　bloom,
That has no flower to lay upon thy tomb!

But from the gladness of the world in May
Death should have called thee on thy destined
　　day,
From joy of singing birds and sun-sweet hours
To some fair grave made beautiful with flowers,
With gentle looks, and tender words to say
Heard long ago, dear brother, of thy song.[1]

---

[1] "A Whisper from the Grave."

Thou should'st have left us when the year was
   young,
Our youngest singer, for thy perfect rest.
Couldst not thou wait till these dark days should
   pass ?
Gracious and sweet and glad thy music was,
Brother, as Spring's, and Spring had mourned
   thee best.

III.

LE CHEVALIER DE CHATELAIN.

FATHER, gone hence, how shall we mourn for
    thee?
Will not some note of triumph break across
Our dirge, some proud strain of our victory
Mix with our lamentation of thy loss?

For lo! the clarions of the dawn are heard
Clear on the hills! Our day, that brings thy night,
Grows splendid with the sunrise at the word
Of Freedom to the world: "Let there be light."

We stand upon the threshold of the day,
Watch the old night dying and the young dawn
    born,
And see the mists and shadows melt away,
And all the world make ready for the morn.

Clear eyes, uplifted to their heaven above,
Pure hands, so strong to labour and to fight,
And proud indignant soul of those who love
The sun, not for his warmth, but for his light!

—O England, whom he loved, whose free shores
        gave
A shelter to his manhood, we will claim
One last gift for him ; give his dust a grave,
And with thy sons remembrance of his name.

And take the loftiest laurels of thy crown
To make a garland for thy dead son's brow
Whom thy hard heart cast forth from thee —
        bend down,
O France, and kiss him—thou art worthy now !

IV.

LOVE, NIGHT, AND DEATH:

IN MEMORY OF RICHARD HENGIST HORNE.

How shall we mourn for our loftiest singer
Gone from the light of the God of song?
Shall Night take gifts that Love would bring her,
And her heart repent her of its wrong,

And let Love pass through the gates of gloom
To speak one word for one ghost to hear—
Only to lay one crown on one tomb,
And only weep but a single tear—

Only to stand by the cold dark River—
Only watch the sail that bears away
From Time to that unknown For Ever
His eyes that look their last on our day—

Only to keep with him, close at his side,
So fain to follow him, loth to stay,
Close at his side, till the ways divide,
And the voice bids part that none gainsay?

Night will not suffer Love to draw near ;
Death bids him back from the gates of gloom ;
Who art thou, Love, and what would'st thou here?
For whom are thy gifts, and thy flowers for whom ?

Love dares not approach the sullen portal,
And lets the lilies fall from his hand ;
His strength is of earth, his wings are mortal
And cannot pass where those warders stand.

Death will not hear, but bids him depart,
And Night will not take the gifts he brings ;
And the chill of Death is in his heart,
And the dews of Night dank on his wings.

Then Love takes back his gifts ungiven,
And leaves the place where his worst foes are,
Night and Death, and looks up to heaven,
And sees the light of his singer's star.[1]

[1] Orion.

V.

LAST WORDS.

DEAF are the ears that heard my song,
Dumb are the lips that praised ;
I shall see them never, my whole life long,
The brave kind eyes upraised
To mine, shall touch not my friend's true hand
Shall see not my friend's true face,
Till I, too, stand in the shadowy land
In my own appointed place.

MADONNA MIA.

" It may be all my love went wrong—
A scribe's work writ awry and blurred
Scrawled after the blind evensong—
Spoilt music with no perfect word.

" But surely I would fain have done
All things the best I could."

MADONNA MIA.

I.

O POOR dead sweet ! I need no more resign
My love and all its privilege of pain,
Seeing none else can come between us twain ;
O love, my love of you has made you mine
For life, and death, and all time : for I know,
For all the doubt that led our lives astray,
For the farewell my lips were loth to say,
For all that God has taken you away,
I never lost you, having loved you so !

And for that shadow of mistrust that came
Between us, and a little set apart
Your soul from mine and heart's faith from my
      heart,
I do not think you were at all to blame ;
I could not set my love beyond the reach

Of little liars to prevent their speech
From mingling with his music, nor some base
Love to make dark the splendour of his face,
And you were sick and sad, weak to believe,
And she, our traitor, cunning to deceive,
And you could know her lie not, for alas,
God set our natures very wide apart
That Love for all his longing could not pass
The great gulf lying between heart and heart ;
You knew me not, but loved me out of sweet
Pure pity of my love, and for your sense
Of noble impulse in me that made beat
My heart to deeper music than most men's.

But since no more again mistrust can fall
Between us, since the past is all forgiven,
Since you have no harsh thought of me in heaven,
But look from God's side, dearest, and know all,
I will not mix *her* name with yours, nor say
Another word of her till in God's sight
I speak before His Judgment-Throne, and pray
For vengeance for my lost life, and the right
She lied from me : to watch you day by day,
To fill your lessening life with growing love,
To be with you till Death came in Love's place,

And that sad solace that she robbed me of,
Your last kiss and the last look of your face !

And O, my sweet, for all my first boy's love
Your own, that first caught passion from your
    face,
And sought the meaning of my life in you,
When all joys of youth's dreams the past denied
In you found their fulfilment, till life knew
The pain of the old longing satisfied,
And found your gladness in the old sorrow's
    place ;

O sweet, for all our baffled lives missed of,
For the division God's harsh hand let fall
Between our souls to part them, O, for all
We might have made each other, for unfaith
Remembered yet forgiven, for your death
That must divide us for a little space,
And for your stainless womanhood that awes
My praises into silence, and because
No stronger, sweeter love may come between
My manhood and your loss, shall fill your place
Quite, or be quite to me what yours had been,
And partly for some little loving speech
Unspoken, some sweet word or deed forgot,

That vex me now you lie beyond their reach :
But chiefly, dearest, that I did you wrong
To blame your woman's weakness with harsh
    thought,
I would your name should hallow my first song.

II.

How will you come to me, fair Love?
  Will you come late or soon?
With sad or smiling skies above,
  By light of sun or moon?

Will you be sad, will you be sweet,
  Sing, sigh, Love, or be dumb?
Will it be summer when we meet,
  Or autumn ere you come?

III.

As one before beginning of the Spring
Feels the changed earth grow sweet with future
    flowers,
And hears in silent woods the glad birds sing,
And sees in winter-time the gracious hours

That bring the greener growth and deeper blue,
So did I know you coming ere you came,
And saw your face in all my dreams of you,
And heard some lovely whispering of your name

In voices of my hopes that had sweet speech
To tell me, O my own, when you were nigh,
And all my thoughts that had some sign to teach
My eager heart that I should know you by ;

For all my days that had no sight of you
By sweet hope of your coming were made fair ;
And long before I saw them, dear, I knew
The perfect colour of your eyes and hair.

IV.

A WOMAN loves me because I love,
And her heart is holy, her soul is pure,
And the stars may change and the firm earth
     move,
But her word remains, and her faith is sure !

Much is to suffer, much is to do,
But my soul is steadfast to feel no fears ;
I know one heart in the world will be true,
One day be sweet of the sorrowful years !

Woes are to bear, and foes not to fear,
And courage to play out a hero's part ;
And songs to sing for the world to hear—-
Then a word to say to a woman's heart !

V.

IF Night might praise the sun, or grief
Sing some sweet song for joy to hear,
Or lonely bird and faded leaf
Praise June, then I might praise you, dear !

VI.

IF words were not so weak
  To tell our best thoughts, dear,
Then I might speak,
  And you might hear !

If Earth were not so bleak,
  Our roses might not die—-
And I might seek
  And find you nigh—

You found, what should I seek ?
  You mine, what should I need
To make this bleak
  Earth Heaven indeed !

VII.

So sweet and sad my lady is, in her
Delight and sorrow hold such equal place,
And either makes her beautiful a space,
That no man knows when she is lovelier,
Whether when she is sorry, or when the rare
Bright smile makes glad her grave and gentle
          face ;
Such gracious sorrow and such sorrowful grace,
In tender interchange make my love fair !

O my one love, whose eyes my spirit sees
In all its dreams, and whose dear face is part
Of all my holier hopes and memories,
To be so good and sweet, no other art,
My gentle Circe, did you use than these,
Nor any magic more to win my heart !

VIII.

O LOVE, this is my own dear lady's praise!
She is so sweet, and good, and pure, and fair,
And has such eyes and gracious-coloured hair,
And sweetness of so beautiful a face,
And is so purely perfect in all ways,
And has such tender mirth, and her glad youth
Smiles in the sweetness of her eyes and mouth,
And lives a life of unembittered days,
And Love could never wish her lovelier,
That a man's life that loved my sweet must be
As hers, so sweet, and good, and pure, and fair—
Dearest, since my own heart has told this me,
O sweet, I only make this only prayer:
Love, give me grace to love you worthily!

IX.

DEAR, your true woman's heart I love you for,
And woman's weaknesses, and hold those eyes
More sweet for their shed tears, and love you
        more
For all your tender insufficiencies.

X.

DEAREST, your life is set so far above
All help of mine, or any need of me,
Being so good and sweet, and could not be
More noble or more happy for my love,

That though I have no hope to keep me true
My life is changed not, nor unfaithful grown—
Sweet, I could only win you for my own
Did you more need me, or I less need you.

XI.

HAD I a heart more like thine own,
   As warm, and kind, and free,
As firm, and fond, thou should'st have known
   That heart but beat for thee !

But since so pure and fair thou art,
   Thou never can'st be mine—
I would not have thee take a heart
   So all unlike from thine !

Thy perfect heart my heart shall teach
   To love thee best of all—
Dear, from thy heaven I cannot reach
   I would not have thee fall !

And what though Fate the gift denies
   Thy heart would not refuse?
Not his the praise who wins the prize,
   But his who dies to lose !

XII.

WITH this fair earth beneath you, these bright
    skies above you
        At rest,
Is not this sweet : to be loved as I love you,
        My best ?

What star shall be ours of all that gleam golden
        Above ?
With what glory enkindled of hope, and beholden
        Of love ?

What souls of true lovers, and poets that sung
    them,
        Shall greet
Your spirit and mine to our own star among them,
        My sweet ?

For I that could give not Love praise, but gave
   duty,
      Unknown,
With these shall have place for the sake of your
   beauty,
      My own !

XIII.

I FEEL the fond clasp of your hand,
And see the true love in your eyes,
Dear love, and once again we stand
And tell to the same stars and skies
What only heaven might understand.

Too high above men's earth, too far
For weak wings of men's words to reach,
Only the soul in yon bright star
Might know the meaning of our speech,
And see our souls, love, as they are.

The lights of the New Day begin
To break ; night's stars fade from the skies ;
Dear Love !   Heaven is not hard to win,
The golden gates of Paradise
Are open : let us enter in !

MADONNA MIA.

II.

I.

I saw fair Love upon an April day,
And Spring had touched his tender lips with red,
And woven a garland for his golden head :
And Hope had taught him such sweet words to
    say
That footsore men upon their weary way
Drew near to listen to what words he said,
And for a little space were comforted—

But on a sudden Love's hands ceased to play
That music that he held not sweet enough,
And from vague impulse touched his instrument
To some strange tune, and at the sound thereof
A bitter pang through all my heart was sent
Until I hid my face and wept, but Love
Played on, and knew not what his playing meant.

II.

IF May forgets not April's flowers,
    June will—
Even hearts as passionate as ours
    Grow still !

July forgets what birds and flowers
    June had—
Even hearts whose joy is deep as ours
    Grow sad !

The pale leaves hear not what the flowers
    Heard told—
Even hearts as passionate as ours
    Grow cold !

III.

HAD you been less harsh with my heart,
Had you suffered my love
To cherish you, tender and true,
To-day had not seen us apart,
Dear love, but for me and for you
How bright had earth been, heaven above
       How blue !

Had you given my heart its will,
Sweet, had you let me speak
All my soul was so fain to say,
The nightingale would be singing still,
And the rose had not died with May,
And these skies had never looked so bleak
       To-day !

IV.

1 SAW in dreams my own love changed and sad
A weary woman, in a pale disguise
Of sunken cheeks and hollow altered eyes,
And all her youth that was so sweet and glad
And all her gracious beauty that she had,
Passed from her in some sorrowful strange wise
And all her voice's music turned to sighs,
And all her body cold and poorly clad.

And then I clasped my poor sweet close to me,
And kissed the wan thin face, and trembling hand,
And told her of our life that I had planned,
How all its lonely longing should be past,
And all its happier hopes should come to be,
Since she was come to love me at the last.

V.

MEN asked us : Will your joy endure,
Your hope betray not nor beguile?
Is Love so strong and Faith so sure?
We only answered with a smile.

Men ask us : Do you still believe
That Love once born can never die,
Nor Faith be false, nor Hope deceive?
We only answer with a sigh.

VI.

HEART of my heart, dear love, as far removed
As this dull earth from yon bright heaven above,
Be loved, if one unloved
    Have grace to love.

Rest, dearest, if the weary can give rest ;
All life's good gifts denied me, sweet, possess—
Be blest, if one unblest
    Have grace to bless.

Live, and forget; though Hope stretch hands
    and call,
You are too far to hear, too far to see—
Live, dear, without me, and God give you all
    He takes from me.

VII.

TILL all is done you would have had me do
  I would not rest—·
Sun, wind, and rain—then nightfall and the dew.
  My best!

BEFORE SUNRISE.

LET none be glad until all are free,
The song be still, and the flag unfurled.
Till all have seen what the poets see,
And foretell to the world.

QUIA MULTUM AMAVI.

I.

WHEN my last hour grows dark for me,
    I shall not fear
Death's dreaded face to see,
    Death's voice to hear.

I shall not fear the night
    When day is done ;
My life was loyal to the light,
    And served the sun.

O brothers, let me rest,
    And think on me,
Whose Love would fain have made you blest,
    Have left you free.

Give me one word of thanks,
    Who fought and died,
Not at your head, yet in your ranks,
    And by your side.

Let Love recall my name,
　　Though Fame forget,
And for the bays I do not claim,
　　O brothers, set

On my remembered grave
　　Our flag I bore—
All I could give your need I gave,
　　Fain to give more!

Let me not wholly die,
　　But Love bid live,
Brothers, though Love was all that I
　　For Love could give.

LOVE, claspt-close in your arms, my head on the
    peace of your breast,
And my mouth against the rose glowing nearest
    your heart at rest,
I dream of the light I leave, and the darkness
    drawing nigh,
As a sick man near to death that watches the
    sunset die.
O Love, I feel you so near that Death must be
    very far !
Is this dim light the dawn, or only the night's
    last star ?
O ! that the might of morning had put the
    shadows to flight,
I would not die in the dark that ever have loved
    the light !

EXPLICIT.

"Yea, the work of our hands, Lord, establish thou
    it !"

CHISWICK PRESS :—C. WHITTINGHAM AND CO.
TOOKS COURT, CHANCERY LANE.